how2become

KS2 MATHS IS EASY

(RATIO, PROPORTION AND ALGEBRA)

THE
REVISION
SERIES

www.How2Become.com

As part of this product you have also received FREE access to online tests that will help you to pass Key Stage 2 MATHS (Ratio, Proportion and Algebra).

To gain access, simply go to:

www.PsychometricTestsOnline.co.uk

Get more products
for passing any test at:

www.how2become.com

Orders: Please contact How2become Ltd, Suite 2, 50 Churchill Square Business Centre, Kings Hill, Kent ME19 4YU.

You can order through Amazon.co.uk under ISBN 9781910602485, via the website www.How2Become.com or through Gardners.com.

ISBN: 9781910602485

First published in 2015 by How2become Ltd.

Typeset for How2become Ltd by Anton Pshinka.

Disclaimer

Every effort has been made to ensure that the information contained within this guide is accurate at the time of publication. How2become Ltd are not responsible for anyone failing any part of any selection process as a result of the information contained within this guide. How2become Ltd and their authors cannot accept any responsibility for any errors or omissions within this guide, however caused. No responsibility for loss or damage occasioned by any person acting, or refraining from action, as a result of the material in this publication can be accepted by How2become Ltd.

The information within this guide does not represent the views of any third party service or organisation.

CONTENTS

THE
REVISION
SERIES

UNDERSTANDING RATIOS

UNDERSTANDING RATIOS

UNDERSTANDING RATIOS

RATIOS compare one part to another part.

Ratios are a great way of comparing numbers.

Example

As shown above, we have 8 squares.

- 5 of the 8 squares are shaded;
- 3 of the 8 squares are white.

If we were to write the ratio of shaded to white squares, we would write it as follows:

5 : 3

> Whatever is written first will be the first number of the ratio! For example, shaded squares are mentioned first, so the first number needs to represent the shaded squares!

Ratios are often written with the use of these two dots.

REMEMBER! The order in which you write the numbers is IMPORTANT. If you switched the order of the numbers around i.e. instead of writing 5 : 3, you wrote 3 : 5, this would mean a different thing.

The use of the two dots between the ratios, basically means 'to every'.

Each ratio represents two parts. These numbers represent different things.

Example contexts:

4 : 2 = Michelle has 4 pink balloons to Mia's 2 balloons.

3 : 5 = Polly has 3 fish to William's 5 fish.

2 : 1 = for every 2 pizzas David buys, Michael buys 1.

Question 1

For the following ratio, come up with a possible context:

3 : 4

Question 2

For the following ratio, come up with a possible context:

2 : 1

Question 3

For the following ratio, come up with a possible context:

5 : 2

Question 4

For the following ratio, come up with a possible context:

10 : 12

Question 5

For the following sentence, write the correct ratio:

Mike has 12 basketballs. Jordan has 3.

☐ : ☐

Question 6

For the following sentence, write the correct ratio:

Sammie eats 7 sweets. Michael eats 9 sweets.

☐ : ☐

Question 7

For the following sentence, write the correct ratio:

For every 6 buttons that Sanjay has, Anil has 15.

☐ : ☐

Question 8

For the following sentence, write the correct ratio:

James has 22 bananas and 13 apples.

☐ : ☐

Question 9

For the following sentence, write the correct ratio:

There are 14 girls and 13 boys in a class.

☐ : ☐

Question 10

For the following sentence, write the correct ratio:

3 Manchester United supporters to every 5 Spurs fans.

☐ : ☐

ANSWERS TO UNDERSTANDING RATIOS

Q1. Your answer could be something like:
'Ollie buys 3 cats. Sam buys 4 dogs'.

Q2. Your answer could be something like:
'Josh buys 2 pencils to every 1 eraser'.

Q3. Your answer could be something like:
'Jane has 5 bracelets to Josie's 2 bracelets'.

Q4. Your answer could be something like:
'I have 10 yellow balls to every 12 green balls'.

Q5. 12 : 3

Q6. 7 : 9

Q7. 6 : 15

Q8. 22 : 13

Q9. 14 : 13

Q10. 3 : 5

HOW ARE YOU GETTING ON?

THE
REVISION
SERIES

RATIOS
OF
SHAPES

RATIOS OF SHAPES

RATIOS OF SHAPES

Ratios are a great way of comparing numbers.

Example 1

What is the ratio of shaded squares to white squares?

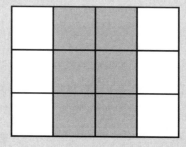

Step 1 = As you can see, there are 12 squares in total.

Step 2 = 6 of the squares are shaded.

Step 3 = So the number of shaded squares to white squares is: 6 : 6.

REMEMBER!

It is important that you write the ratio in order of what it is asking for in the question.

- So in the above example, the question is asking the ratio of shaded squares to white squares. Therefore the number of shaded squares should be written first.

Question 1

Work out the ratio of white triangles to shaded triangles.

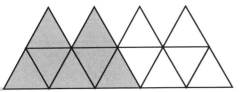

Question 2

Work out the ratio of shaded segments to white segments.

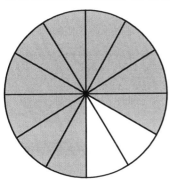

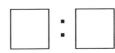

Question 3

Work out the ratio of shaded triangles to white triangles.

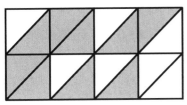

☐ : ☐

Question 4

Work out the ratio of white rectangles to shaded rectangles.

☐ : ☐

Question 5

Shade in the squares so that the ratio of shaded to white squares is **5 : 3.**

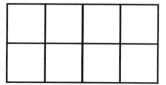

Question 6

Shade in the squares so that the ratio of white to shaded squares is **2 : 7.**

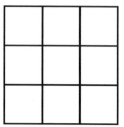

Question 7

Shade in the rectangles so that the ratio of white to shaded rectangles is **6 : 2**

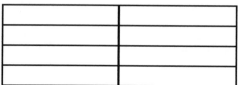

Question 8

Shade in the squares so that the ratio of white to shaded squares is **7 : 13.**

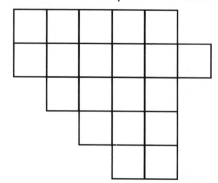

ANSWERS TO RATIOS OF SHAPES

Q1. 6 : 7

EXPLANATION = there are 6 white triangles, and 7 shaded triangles.

Q2. 10 : 2

EXPLANATION = there are 10 shaded segments, and 2 white segments.

Q3. 9 : 7

EXPLANATION = there are 9 shaded triangles, and 7 white triangles.

Q4. 4 : 1

EXPLANATION = there are 4 white rectangles, and 1 shaded rectangle.

Q5. Your answer should look something like this:

Q6. Your answer should look something like this:

Q7. Your answer should look something like this:

Q8. Your answer should look something like this:

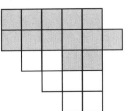

HOW ARE YOU GETTING ON?

THE
REVISION
SERIES

SIMPLIFYING AND EQUIVALENT RATIOS

SIMPLIFYING AND EQUIVALENT RATIOS

EQUIVALENT RATIOS

The word **EQUIVALENT** in terms of ratios means to find other ratios that are *'equal to'* the original ratio.

You can find equivalent ratios by one simple method:

- Equivalent ratios can be found by **multiplying** or **dividing** the two parts of the ratio by the **same** number.

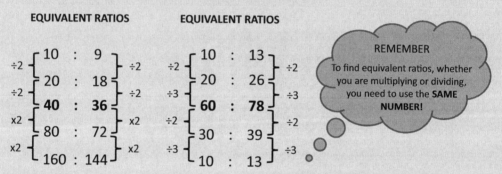

EQUIVALENT RATIOS

÷2	10 : 9	÷2
÷2	20 : 18	÷2
	40 : 36	
x2	80 : 72	x2
x2	160 : 144	x2

EQUIVALENT RATIOS

÷2	10 : 13	÷2
÷2	20 : 26	÷3
÷3	**60 : 78**	
÷2	30 : 39	÷2
÷3	10 : 13	÷3

REMEMBER

To find equivalent ratios, whether you are multiplying or dividing, you need to use the **SAME NUMBER!**

Now you try!

Using the ratio below, list 6 different equivalent ratios.

50 : 25

Using the ratio below, list 6 different equivalent ratios.

120 : 80

SIMPLIFYING AND EQUIVALENT RATIOS

SIMPLIFYING RATIOS

The word **SIMPLIFYING** simply means 'to make simple'. Sometimes, you can simplify ratios in order to make them easier to understand.

You can simplify ratios using one easy method: **TIP**

- Find a number that can be divided into both numbers, until the two parts of the ratio can no longer be divided by the same number.

EXAMPLE

Write the following ratio in its simplest form.

12 : 8

Step 1 = you need to find a number that can be divided into '12' and '8'.

Step 2 = both numbers are even, so let's start by dividing both numbers by **2.**

$$12 \div 2 = 6$$
$$8 \div 2 = 4$$

Step 3 = so now you have the ratio 6 : 4.

Step 4 = both numbers are still even, so let's divide by 2 again.

$$6 \div 2 = 3$$
$$4 \div 2 = 2$$

Step 5 = now we have the ratio 3 : 2.

Step 6 = we cannot simplify this any more because 3 is a prime number, and no other numbers can be divided into 3.

12 : 8 6 : 4 3 : 2

Now you try!

Write the following ratio in its simplest form:

24 : 18

Question 1

Lalita needs your help. Below there are 10 cards. Each card has a ratio. Help Lalita match the equivalent boxes from the top row to the bottom row. The first one has been done for you.

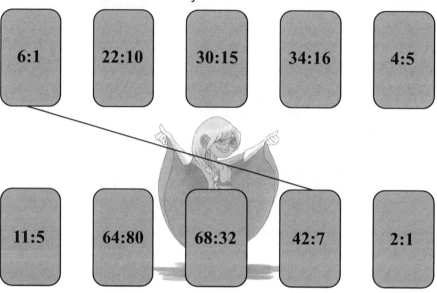

Question 2

Complete the following ratios by making them equivalent to the ratio **60 : 100**.

a) ☐ : **50**

b) **6** : ☐

c) **15** : ☐

d) ☐ : **20**

e) **3** : ☐

f) ☐ : **300**

Question 3

Lalita needs your help. She wants to put these ratios in their simplest form. Can you help?

a) **4 : 16**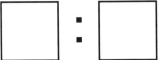

b) **70 : 20**

c) **64 : 32**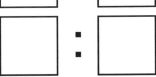

Question 4

If the statement is true, put a ✔ in the box. If the statement is false, put a ✘ in the box.

a) 4 : 3 is equivalent to 16 : 12.

b) 12 : 6 in its simplest form is 1 : 2.

c) 24 : 11 is already in its simplest form.

d) 50 grams of flour, 40 grams of sugar and 100 grams of butter. In its simplest form, this would be 5 : 4 : 1.

Question 5

To make up blackcurrant squash, you will need to use the blackcurrant squash and the water in the ratio of 1 : 3 (in order to make up 1 litre). With this in mind, calculate how much of each ingredient you will need to make up the following. Write your answers as a ratio.

a) 4 litres of blackcurrant squash = _____

b) 20 litres of blackcurrant squash = _____

c) 34 litres of blackcurrant squash = _____

Question 6

Lalita earns £460 in one week. Her friend Freddie earns £600 in a week. What is the ratio of Lalita's to Freddie's earnings? In its simplest form.

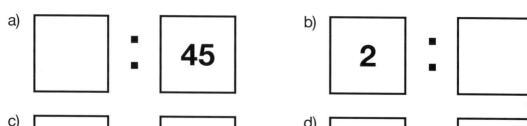

Question 7

Complete the following simplified ratios by making them equivalent to the ratio **36 : 90**.

a) ☐ : 45

b) 2 : ☐

c) 6 : ☐

d) ☐ : 30

Question 8

Write the following ratios in their simplest form.

a) 15 : 5

b) 40 : 10

c) 12 : 18

_____

_____

_____

d) 35 : 5

e) 6 : 3

f) 48 : 56

_____

_____

_____

ANSWERS TO SIMPLIFYING AND EQUIVALENT RATIOS

Q1. Your answer should look like this:

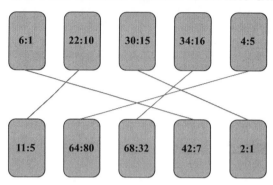

Q2. a) 30 : 50

EXPLANATION = both 60 and 100 can be divided by 2.

b) 6 : 10

EXPLANATION = both 60 and 100 can be divided by 10.

c) 15 : 25

EXPLANATION = both 60 and 100 can be divided by 4.

d) 12 : 20

EXPLANATION = both 60 and 100 can be divided by 5.

e) 3 : 5

EXPLANATION = both 60 and 100 can be divided by 20.

f) 180 : 300

EXPLANATION = both 60 and 100 can be multiplied by 3.

Q3. a) 1 : 4

EXPLANATION = 4 : 16 can be simplified to 1 : 4. Both numbers can be divided by 4.

b) 7 : 2

EXPLANATION = 70 : 20 can be simplified to 7 : 2. Both numbers can be divided by 10.

c) 2 : 1

EXPLANATION = 64 : 32 can be simplified to 2 : 1. Both numbers can be divided by 32.

Q4. a) ✔

EXPLANATION = 4 : 3 is equivalent to 16 : 12, Both numbers have been multiplied by 4.

b) ✘

EXPLANATION = 1 : 2 is not the simplest form of 12 : 6. Instead is should be 2 : 1, not 1 : 2.

c) ✔

EXPLANATION = 24 : 11 is already in its simplest form because 11 is a prime number, and therefore no numbers can be divided into it.

d) ✘

EXPLANATION = 50 : 40 : 100 in its simplest form would be 5 : 4 : 10, not 5 : 4 : 1.

Q5. a) 4 : 12

EXPLANATION = both parts of the ratio (1 and 3) need to be multiplied by 4.

b) 20 : 60

EXPLANATION = both parts of the ratio (1 and 3) need to be multiplied by 20.

c) 34 : 102

EXPLANATION = both parts of the ratio (1 and 3) need to be multiplied by 34.

Q6. 23 : 30

EXPLANATION = the ratio of Lalita's and Freddie's money is 460 : 600. This can be simplified to 23 : 30. Both 460 and 600 can be divided by 20.

Q7. a) 18 : 45
b) 2 : 5
c) 6 : 15
d) 12 : 30

Q8. a) 3 : 1
b) 4 : 1
c) 2 : 3
d) 7 : 1
e) 2 : 1
f) 6 : 7

HOW ARE YOU GETTING ON?

THE
REVISION
SERIES

RATIO, PROPORTION AND FRACTIONS

RATIO, PROPORTION AND FRACTIONS

We have already spent some time learning about ratios. However, another key thing that you will be expected to know is **proportion**.

REMEMBER

Ratio and proportion **are not** the same!

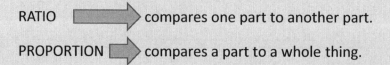

RATIO ➡ compares one part to another part.

PROPORTION ➡ compares a part to a whole thing.

Ratios

Ratios use dots (:) to compare two parts. Words that are often used in terms of ratio are:

- "for every";
- "to".

Example

> The ratio of white rabbits **to** black rabbits is 1 : 3.

Proportion

Proportions are very similar to fractions. Instead of comparing two parts, you are comparing one part with the whole product/object.

Example

> Let's say you had 8 boxes. 2 of the boxes are empty and 6 of them are full. Now the ratio of empty to full boxes can be written as 2 : 6 or 1 : 3.
>
> ➤ The **proportion** of empty boxes is 2 in every 8 boxes.
> ➤ The **proportion** of full boxes is 6 in every 8 boxes.

Can you see, with proportions the last number will be the **whole** of something i.e. all of the boxes, whereas ratio breaks up the whole thing, and puts it in two. These two parts, when added together, would add up to the whole thing.

RATIO, PROPORTION AND FRACTIONS

PROPORTION AND FRACTION

Take a look at the following shape:

The proportion of shaded rectangles is 3 in every 9 (or 1 in 3).
This can also be written as $^3/_9$ or $^1/_3$.

By simply using the above example, we can see that:

- The **proportion** of shaded rectangles is 3 out of 9.
- The **proportion** of white rectangles is 6 out of 9.
- The **ratio** of shaded to white rectangles would be 3 : 6.
- The **fraction** of white rectangles is 6/9 or 2/3.

Now you try!
Use the shape below to answer the following questions.

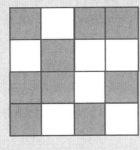

The **fraction** of shaded squares is:

The **proportion** of white squares is:

The **ratio** of white to shaded squares is:

Question 1

Look at the stars below, and answer the following questions.

a) What is the ratio of white to shaded stars?

$\boxed{} : \boxed{}$

b) How many stars are shaded? Write your answer as a
    fraction and in its simplest form.

$\dfrac{\boxed{}}{\boxed{}}$

Question 2

The proportion of girls to boys in a classroom is 3 : 4. How many girls are
there in the class, if the class has 28 pupils?

Question 3

If a proportion represents "4 in every 9", what is this written

as a fraction?

$\dfrac{\boxed{}}{\boxed{}}$

Question 4

Lalita and her friend Scarlett are sharing sweets in the ratio 2 : 3. If Scarlett eats 15 sweets, what was the total number of sweets?

Question 5

Explain the difference between ratio and proportion, using examples to support your answer.

_____

_____

_____

_____

Question 6

Below are two different sized balloons. Carefully study the balloons and answer the following question.

What is the ratio of small balloons to big balloons?

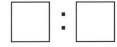

Question 7

Match the fractions with the equivalent proportions. The first one has been done for you.

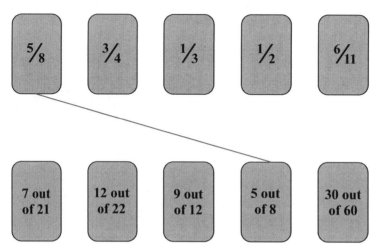

Question 8

Write down all of the simplified ratios that are equivalent to 50 : 60.

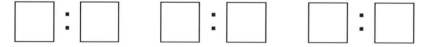

Question 9

For every six slices of pizza Joey eats, Tom eats 2. This amounts to a whole pizza.

a) How much of the total pizza does Tom eat? Write your answer as a fraction and in its simplest form.

---

b) What proportion of pizza does Tom eat?

ANSWERS TO RATIO, PROPORTION AND FRACTIONS

Q1. a) 12 : 12 or 1 : 1

EXPLANATION = there are the same amount of white stars as there are shaded stars. There are 12 white stars and 12 shaded stars. This can be simplified to 1 : 1.

b) 1/2

EXPLANATION = half of the overall total of stars are shaded.

Q2. 12

EXPLANATION = the class has 28 pupils altogether. So 28 ÷ 7 (the total ratio) x 3 (the number of girls) = 12. So, in a class of 28 pupils, there would be 12 girls and 16 boys.

Q3. 4/9

EXPLANATION = remember, proportions are just another way of writing a fraction. Therefore 4 in every 9, would simply be 4/9.

Q4. 25

EXPLANATION = the ratio of sweets is split 2 : 3 (5 in total). Scarlett eats 15. So 15 ÷ 3 = 5. So Lalita must have had 5 x 2 = 10 sweets. So 15 + 10 = 25 sweets in total.

Q5. Your answer should read something like this:

'Ratio compares one part to another part, whereas proportions compare a part with the whole of something. For example, if there were 3 red buttons and 7 green buttons, the ratio of red to green buttons would be 3 : 7. If we were trying to find the proportion of red buttons, then we would say that 3 out of the 10 buttons are red.'

Q6. 7 : 4

EXPLANATION = there are 7 small balloons and 4 big balloons.

Q7. Your answer should look like this:

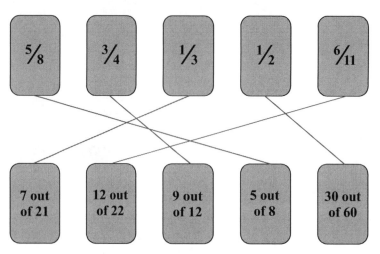

Q8. 25 : 30

10 : 12

5 : 6

Q9. a) ¼

EXPLANATION = Joey eats 6 slices and Tom eats 2 = that means there are 8 slices that make up the pizza. Tom eats 2, and this as a fraction is 2/8 or 1/4

b) 2 out of 8

EXPLANATION = Tom eats 2 slices out of the 8 total slices.

HOW ARE YOU GETTING ON?

THE
REVISION
SERIES

RATIO AND PROPORTION PROBLEMS

RATIO AND PROPORTION PROBLEMS

We have already spent some time learning about ratios and proportions.

You may be given questions that require you to work out a problem using ratios and proportions.

These will require you to understand ratios and proportions in order to solve the problems.

REMEMBER!

- Pick out the key information from the problem.
- Some of the information in the problem will be worded so that it makes it seem more confusing.
- However if you take out all of the relevant information, the problem will become much clearer.

EXAMPLE

There are 24 red balls and the rest are blue. The ratio of red balls to blue balls is 4 : 6. How many blue balls are there?

Step 1 = the ratio 4 : 6 means 'there are 4 red balls to every 6 blue balls'.

Step 2 = so 24 ÷ 4 = 6

Step 3 = to work out the number of blue balls, 6 x 6 = 36.

Step 4 = there are 36 blue balls.

Question 1

Lalita wants your help. She is making strawberry ice cream from scratch. Below are the ingredients she will need, catering for 4 people.

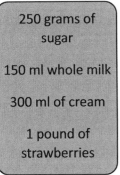

250 grams of sugar

150 ml whole milk

300 ml of cream

1 pound of strawberries

How much of each ingredient will Lalita need if she wanted to make ice cream for 12 people?

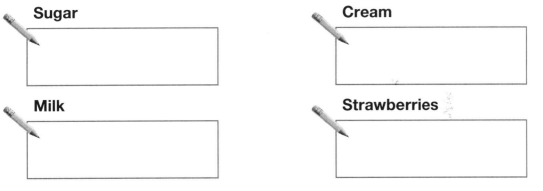

Sugar

Cream

Milk

Strawberries

Question 2

Emma and Amanda are given £600. They have agreed to split the money in the ratio of 2 : 3. How much money will each person get?

Emma

Amanda

Question 3

Shade in the correct number of marbles, so that the ratio of white to shaded marbles is 5 : 6.

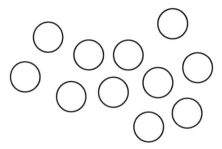

Question 4

Using the above question, what is the proportion of shaded marbles?

Question 5

You visit an animal sanctuary. The sanctuary contains 48 giraffes and 64 monkeys. What is the ratio of giraffes to monkeys, in its simplest form?

Question 6

Elizabeth works on a farm. She finds that 336 of her eggs are either broken or spoiled. The rest of her eggs are in good condition, and she will be able to sell them. In its simplest form, what is the ratio of bad eggs to good eggs, if she has 1,200 eggs in total?

☐ : ☐

Question 7

Below is a list of proportions and ratios. Match these to their equivalent fraction. We have done the first one for you.

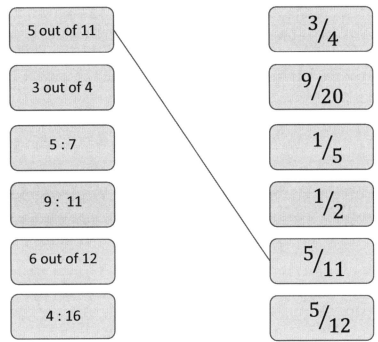

5 out of 11	$^3/_4$
3 out of 4	$^9/_{20}$
5 : 7	$^1/_5$
9 : 11	$^1/_2$
6 out of 12	$^5/_{11}$
4 : 16	$^5/_{12}$

Question 8

Lalita and Preston both take a trip at different times. The distance travelled by Lalita and Preston can be put in the ratio 4 : 7. If Preston travelled 63 miles, how many miles did Lalita travel on her journey?

Question 9

Below is a rectangle. The ratio of the sides of the shape is 2 : 4. The shape is scaled up using a factor of 6.

What are the new side lengths of the rectangle? Write your answer in centimetres.

2cm

4cm

Question 10

Jamie's favourite chocolate is smarties. He only eats the red, yellow, green and orange ones. The ratio of these colour smarties are in the ratio 2 : 3 : 1 : 2

Jamie picks out all the smarties that he eats and is left with 72 (of the colours that he eats). Write down how many of each colour of the smarties Jamie has.

a) Red

b) Yellow

c) Green

d) Orange

ANSWERS TO RATIO AND PROPORTION PROBLEMS

Q1. Sugar = 750g

Cream = 900 ml

Milk = 450 ml

Strawberries = 3 pounds

All you need to do is to multiply the original ingredients by 3. (There are 3 times the number of people you need to cater for, so you need 3 times more ingredients).

Q2. Emma = £240, Amanda = £360

EXPLANATION = Emma = 600 ÷ 5 x 2 = £240

Amanda = 600 ÷ 5 x 3 = £360

Q3. Your marbles should look something like this:

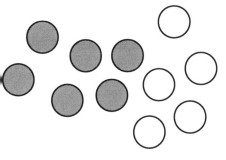

Q4. The proportion of shaded marbles is 6 in every 11

EXPLANATION = remember proportions compare one part to the overall total (i.e. the whole).

Q5. ¾

EXPLANATION = 48 giraffes and 64 monkeys. This can be simplified to ¾. Both 48 and 64 can be divided by 16.

Q6. 7 : 18

EXPLANATION = there are 1,200 eggs in total. 336 are bad eggs, which means 1,200 – 336 = 864 (good eggs). Therefore the ratio is 336 : 864. This can be simplified to 7 : 18. (Both 336 and 864 can be divided by 48).

Q7. Your answer should look something like this:

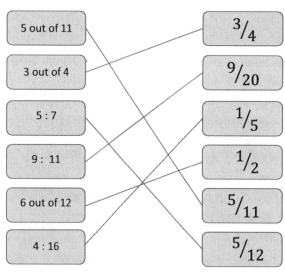

5 out of 11	$3/4$
3 out of 4	$9/20$
5 : 7	$1/5$
9 : 11	$1/2$
6 out of 12	$5/11$
4 : 16	$5/12$

Q8. 36 miles

EXPLANATION = Preston travelled 63 miles. The ratio of Lalita to Preston's distance travelled is 4 : 7. So, 63 ÷ 7 = 9.

So, 9 x 4 = 36 miles (Lalita's distance travelled).

Q9. 12 cm and 24 cm

EXPLANATION = the rectangle is scaled up by a factor of 6. So 2 : 4 needs to be multiplied by 6 (on both sides).

2 x 6 = 12 cm

4 x 6 = 24 cm

Q10. a) 18

EXPLANATION = 72 ÷ 8 x 2 = 18

   b) 27

EXPLANATION = 72 ÷ 8 x 3 = 27

   c) 9

EXPLANATION = 72 ÷ 8 x 1 = 9

   d) 18

EXPLANATION = 72 ÷ 8 x 2 = 18

HOW ARE YOU GETTING ON?

THE
REVISION
SERIES

UNDERSTANDING ALGEBRA

UNDERSTANDING ALGEBRA

UNDERSTANDING ALGEBRA

Instead of using numbers to solve math problems, sometimes you will be given letters and symbols to work out a mathematical equation. This is known as **algebra**.

In order to work out algebra:

- You need to be able to work out what the letters and/or symbols represent. Without knowing what they represent, you will struggle to work out the correct answers.

EXAMPLE

Let's write out the first 10 digits.

$$1 \quad 2 \quad 3 \quad 4 \quad 5 \quad 6 \quad 7 \quad 8 \quad 9 \quad 10$$

Now these numbers could be represented using letters:

1 = a

2 = b

3 = c

4 = d

5 = e

6 = f

7 = g

8 = h

9 = i

10 = j

Question 1

b + f
Step 1 = b (2) + f (6) = 8

Question 2

i ÷ c
Step 1 = i (9) ÷ c (3) = 3

Question 3

j x g
Step 1 = j (10) x g (7) = 70

The above is very basic, but hopefully gives you some idea of what we mean by **algebra**.

UNDERSTANDING ALGEBRA

THE BASICS

As shown on the previous page, letters are often used instead of numbers.

These letters represent a number, and your task is to work out what that number is.

A key thing to remember:

- If there is a number next to a letter, i.e. without a space, that means you will need to multiply that letter and the number together.

EXAMPLE

Let's write out the first 10 digits.

1   2   3   4   5   6   7   8   9   10

Now these numbers could be represented using letters:

1 = a

2 = b

3 = c

4 = d

5 = e

6 = f

7 = g

8 = h

9 = i

10 = j

Question 1

3c + d
Step 1 = 3c *(3 x 3)* + d *(4)* = 9 + 4 = 13

Question 2

7b ÷ b
Step 1 = 7b *(7 x 2)* ÷ b *(2)* = 14 ÷ 2 = 7

Question 3

9c x e
Step 1 = 9c *(9 x 3)* x e *(5)* = 135

Again, these are very basic algebra equations, but you need to be able to grasp the concept of these first, before attempting harder questions.

UNDERSTANDING ALGEBRA

LETTERS AND SYMBOLS

In algebra, letters and symbols are often used to replace numbers.

It doesn't matter what the symbol is, what does matter is what it stands for.

USING SYMBOLS

Sometimes a symbol will be used instead of a number.

7 + ☆ = 15   ☆ = [   ]

Step 1 = the star represents a number. You need to work out what that number is.

Step 2 = if 7 + ☆ = 15, that means that 15 – 7 = 8. (Because the equation is an addition, in order to work out the value of the star, you must do the opposite operation, and in this case it is subtraction).

Step 3 = 8 is the value of the star. If we factor that into the equation:

$$7 + 8 = 15$$

USING LETTERS

Just like symbols, letters can be used in the very same way.

19 - m = 6 m = [   ]

Step 1 = the 'm' represents a number. You need to work out what that number is.
Step 2 = if 19 - m = 6, that means that 19 - 6 = 13.
Step 3 = 13 is the value of the letter 'm'. If we factor that into the equation:

$$19 - 13 = 6$$

When using letters and symbols in equations, these are also known as **expressions***. I will discuss expressions in the next chapter.*

Question 1

If **a = 6, b = 4** and **c = 2**, work out the following equations:

a) **2b + c**

b) **6 + bc**

c) **2b − c**

d) **2a + 3b + c**

e) **7c − a**

f) **9b ÷ a**

Question 2

Simplify the following equations:

a) **c + c + c + a**

b) **d + d + d − d**

c) **a x c x c x a**

d) **(a + a + a + a) x (c + c + c)**

e) **5 x d**

f) **b + b + b − c**

Question 3

Work out the following symbols.

a) 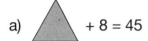 + 8 = 45

△ = [ ]

b) ⌐ x 4 = 28

⌐ = [ ]

c) 36 ÷ ○ = 12

○ = [ ]

d) 121 - ⬇ = 56

⬇ = [ ]

Question 4

Work out the following letters.

a) $35 - t = 17$

$t =$ [ ]

b) $r \div 5 = 8$

$r =$ [ ]

c) $n^2 = 49$

$n =$ [ ]

d) $k + 6 - 3 = 15$

$k =$ [ ]

e) $6h = 90$

$h =$ [ ]

f) $(4 \times m) + (m^2) = 60$

$m =$ [ ]

ANSWERS TO UNDERSTANDING ALGEBRA

Q1. a) 10
EXPLANATION = 2b (2 x 4) + 2
8 + 2 = 10

 b) 14
EXPLANATION = 6 + bc (4 x 2)
6 + 8 = 14

 c) 6
EXPLANATION = 2b (2 x 4) – 2
8 – 2 = 6

 d) 26
EXPLANATION = 2a (2 x 6) + 3b (3 x 4) + 2
12 + 12 + 2 = 26

 e) 8
EXPLANATION = 7c (7 x 2) – 6
14 – 6 = 8

 f) 6
EXPLANATION = 9b (9 x 4) ÷ 6
36 ÷ 6 = 6

Q2. a) 3c + a
EXPLANATION = c + c + c (3c) + a

 b) 2d
EXPLANATION = d + d + d (3d) – d = 2d

 c) 2a x 2c
EXPLANATION = a x c x c x a (2a x 2c)

 d) 4a x 3c
EXPLANATION = a + a + a + a (4a) x c + c + c (3c)

 e) 5d
EXPLANATION = 5 x d = 5d

 f) 3b – c
EXPLANATION = b + b + b (3b) – c

Q3. a) ▲ = 37

EXPLANATION = 37 + 8 = 45 (45 − 8 = 37)

b) ⌐ = 7

EXPLANATION = 7 x 4 = 28 (28 ÷ 4 = 7)

c) ○ = 3

EXPLANATION = 36 ÷ 3 = 12 (36 ÷ 12 = 3)

d) ⬇ = 65

EXPLANATION = 121 − 65 = 56 (121 − 56 = 65)

Q4. a) *t* = 18

EXPLANATION = 35 − 18 = 17 (35 − 17 = 18)

b) *r* = 40

EXPLANATION = 40 ÷ 5 = 8 (5 x 8 = 40)

c) *n* = 7

EXPLANATION = 7 x 7 = 49 (square root of 49 = 7)

d) *k* = 12

EXPLANATION = 12 + 6 − 3 = 15 (6 − 3 = 3, 15 − 3 = 12)

e) *h* = 15

EXPLANATION = 6 x 15 = 90 (90 ÷ 6 = 15)

f) *m* = 6

EXPLANATION = (4 x 6 = 24) + (6 x 6 = 36)   24 + 36 = 60

HOW ARE YOU GETTING ON?

ALGEBRA — FORMULAS AND EXPRESSIONS

ALGEBRA – FORMULAS AND EXPRESSIONS

UNDERSTANDING FORMULA

Formulas are a great way to write something in a short way.

SYMBOLS = can be used to replace numbers. These symbols will represent a number.

LETTERS = can also be used instead of numbers and symbols. You will be asked to work out the value of that letter.

LETTER FORMULA = will usually shorten the equation down by writing the expression using letters and symbols.

EXPRESSION = an expression uses both letters and numbers but does not contain an equals sign.

EQUATION = an equation uses both letters and numbers but does contain an equals sign.

SOME FORMULAS MEAN THE SAME THING

Some formulas look different but are ACTUALLY the same.

Let's take the number **7**. This can be represented in many different ways:

- 7
- 1 + 6
- 2 + 5
- 3 + 4

This is the same for working with letters. If you have **3 x n**, this is the same as **3n**.

Remember this when you are using different formulas!

ALGEBRA – FORMULAS AND EXPRESSIONS

USING FORMULAS TO FIND SHAPE MEASUREMENTS

When it comes to working out shape measurements, using formula is a great way to understand things in a simpler way.

BASIC SHAPE FORMULAS

PERIMETER OF A SQUARE

P (perimeter) = 4L (lengths)

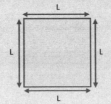

EXAMPLE

If each length of the square was 8cm, then the perimeter of the square would be:

$$8 + 8 + 8 + 8 = 32$$

AREA OF A SQUARE

A (area) = **b** (base) x **h** (height)

EXAMPLE

If each length of the square was 10cm, then the area of the square would be:

$$10 \times 10 = 100$$

AREA OF A TRIANGLE

A (area) = **½hb** (height x base)

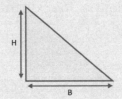

EXAMPLE

If the height of the triangle was 8, and the base of the triangle was 4:

$$8 \times 4 = 32$$
$$32 \div 2 = 16$$

Question 1

Lalita needs your help. Using the correct formula, work out the area of the shape below. We have provided space for you to write out the correct formula and write the correct answer.

12cm

8cm

Answer:

Question 2

The area of a triangle has the equation **A = ½ bh. A** is the area of the triangle, **b** is the base of the triangle and the **h** is the height of the triangle. If the height of the triangle is 11cm, and the base is 5cm, what is the area of the triangle?

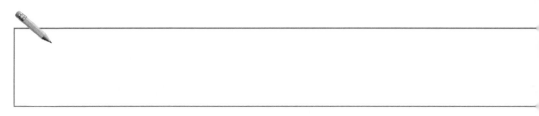

Question 3

The area of a square has the equation **A = bh. A** is the area of the square, **b** is the base of the square and the **h** is the height of the square. If the height of the square is 9cm, and the base is 9cm what is the area of the square?

Question 4

Match up all of the expressions that mean the same thing. The expressions can have more than one match.

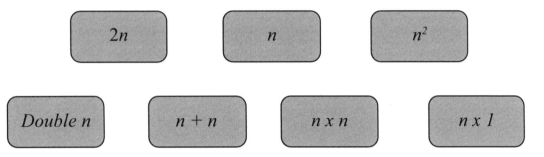

Question 5

Ellie goes to an Italian restaurant. A pizza slice costs £0.75 and chips cost £1.50. Write an equation for the price of Ellie's dinner if she eats 1 portion of chips and **N** amount of pizza slices.

Question 6

Freddie goes into an ice cream store. A scoop of ice cream costs £0.85. Write down the formula in words and in letters for the cost **C**, of the number of scoops **S** of ice cream.

FORMULA IN WORDS:

FORMULA IN LETTERS:

Question 7

Complete the following table.

n	6*n*	5*n* - 2	7*n* + 3
4			
	12		
		23	

Question 8

A strawberry cake costs £1.75. Write a formula to show the total cost of buying x amount of cakes.

Question 9

The formula for the number of raisins in a cookie is = Number of raisins = 6 x number of cookies.

If there are 12 cookies in total, how many raisins are there altogether?

Question 10

Vincent has the expression 9n ÷ 5. If the total is 9, what is the value of the term n?

ANSWERS TO ALGEBRA – FORMULAS AND EXPRESSIONS

Q1. 96 cm²

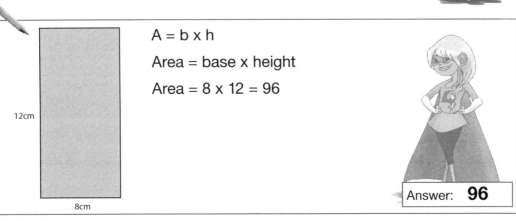

12cm

8cm

$A = b \times h$

Area = base x height

Area = 8 x 12 = 96

Answer: **96**

Q2. 27.5 cm²

EXPLANATION = 11 x 5 = 55

55 ÷ 2 = 27.5

Q3. 81 cm²

EXPLANATION = 9 x 9 = 81 cm²

Q4. Your answer should look something like this:

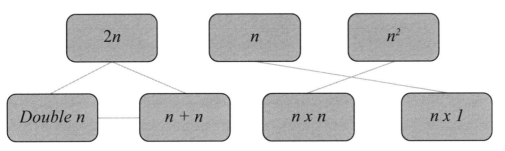

$2n$ n n^2

Double n $n + n$ $n \times n$ $n \times 1$

Q5. C = 1.50 + 0.75n

EXPLANATION = C (total cost) = 1.50 (the price of the chips) + 0.75n (the number of pizza slices that are ordered).

Q6. In words = the total cost is the number of ice cream scoops multiplied by the cost per scoop, which is 0.85p.

In letters = C = 0.85s (cost = price x number of scoops)

EXPLANATION = pay attention to what the letters are representing in the situation. If you understand what the letter is representing, these questions will become relatively simple.

Q7. Your answer should look like this:

n	$6n$	$5n - 2$	$7n + 3$
4	24	18	31
2	12	8	17
5	30	23	38

Q8. Total cost = 1.75 x number of cakes

EXPLANATION = you will need to multiply the cost per cake by the number of cakes.

Q9. 72

EXPLANATION = 6 x 12 = 72

Q10. n = 5

EXPLANATION = 9 x 5 = 45 ÷ 5 = 9

HOW ARE YOU GETTING ON?

THE
REVISION
SERIES

ALGEBRA – SUBSTITUTING LETTERS FOR NUMBERS

ALGEBRA – SUBSTITUTING LETTERS FOR NUMBERS

SUBSTITUTING LETTERS FOR NUMBERS

When it comes to numbers, letters and algebra, we know that the letters in an equation are used to represent numbers.

Instead of working out what the letter is as a number, sometimes you may be given a question that already gives you the value of the letters, and you simply need to work out the sum.

EXAMPLE

Work out $3x + 4y$, when $x = 4$, and $y = 2$

Step 1 = you are already given the values of x and y, so now you just need to do the calculation.

Step 2 = remember, when you have a number in front of a letter, that means you must multiply the number by the value of the letter.

Step 3 = if $x = 4$

$$3 \times 4 = 12$$

Step 4 = if $y = 2$

$$4 \times 2 = 8$$

Step 5 = $12 + 8 = 20$

Step 6 = so the correct answer is 20.

Now you try!

Work out the following expressions.

$4x \div 3y$	$7x + 4y$
$x = 6$ and $y = 2$	$x = 5$ and $y = 2$

Question 1

Find $4a + 8b$, if $a = 5$ and $b = 4$.

Question 2

Find $6a + 3e$, if $a = 3$ and $e = 9$.

Question 3

Find $8x - 4y$, if $x = 4$ and $y = 2$.

Question 4

Find $4a \times 6b$, if $a = 3$ and $b = 2$.

Question 5

Find $6y \div 3z$, if $y = 4$ and $z = 1$.

Question 6

Find $4x - 3y$, if $x = 4$ and $y = 2$.

Question 7

Find $4x - 3y$, if $x = 4$ and $y = -2$.

Question 8

Find $4a - 2b - 3c$, when $a = 9$, $b = 3$ and $c = 2$.

Question 9

Find $20y - 8x$, if $y = 5$ and $x = 3$.

Question 10

Find $n^2 + 8y + 3z$, if $n = 6$, $y = 2$, $z = 4$.

ANSWERS TO ALGEBRA – SUBSTITUTING LETTERS FOR NUMBERS

Q1. 52

EXPLANATION = (4 x 5 = 20) + (8 x 4 = 32).

20 + 32 = 52

Q2. 45

EXPLANATION = (6 x 3 = 18) + (3 x 9 = 27)

18 + 27 = 45

Q3. 24

EXPLANATION = (8 x 4 = 32) – (4 x 2 = 8)

32 – 8 = 24

Q4. 144

EXPLANATION = (4 x 3 = 12) x (6 x 2 = 12)

12 x 12 = 144

Q5. 8

EXPLANATION = (6 x 4 = 24) ÷ (3 x 1 = 3)

24 ÷ 3 = 8

Q6. 10

EXPLANATION = (4 x 4 = 16) - (3 x 2 = 6)

16 - 6 = 10

Q7. 22

EXPLANATION = (4 x 4 = 16) - (3 x -2 = -6)

16 - -6 = 16 + 6 = 22

Q8. 24

EXPLANATION = (4 x 9 = 36) – (2 x 3 = 6) – (3 x 2 = 6)

36 – 6 – 6 = 24

Q9. 76

EXPLANATION = (20 x 5 = 100) – (8 x 3 = 24)

100 – 24 = 76

Q10. 64

EXPLANATION = (6^2 = 6 x 6 = 36) + (8 x 2 = 16) + (3 x 4 = 12)

36 + 16 + 12 = 64

THE
REVISION
SERIES

ALGEBRA –
FORMING
EXPRESSIONS

ALGEBRA – FORMING EXPRESSIONS

FORMING EXPRESSIONS

REMEMBER – expressions are just lines of algebra that contain letters.

Whilst you may not be asked to form an expression yourself, understanding how to do so will greatly improve your understanding of using expressions and what they represent.

EXAMPLE

Freddie goes to football practice three times a week and it costs X amount of pounds.

Freddie is also part of an ice-hockey team which he attends twice a week, which costs Y amount of pounds.

<u>Write the above information as an expression for the total cost per week.</u>

Step 1 = for this question, you are working out the expression which will demonstrate the total cost spent on Freddie's weekly activities.

Step 2 = Freddie plays football 3 times a week. This can be represented as follows:

$3x$ (x is the amount it costs, and 3 is the number of times he plays).

Step 3 = Freddie attends ice hockey practice 2 times a week. This can be represented as follows:

$2y$ (y is the amount it costs, and 2 is the number of times he attends practice).

Step 4 = therefore the expression can be written as follows:

$3x + 2y$

Question 1

Sammie has *A* amount of marbles. He loses 6 of them.

Write the expression to show how many marbles Sammie is now left with.

Question 2

It is Lalita's birthday, and her mum and dad have just bought her two kittens. Lalita is told that she needs to buy a bed for each cat (*B*) and 14 packets of cat food (*F*) per week, per kitten.

For the two beds, and the number of packets of cat food that Lalita needs to buy per week per kitten, write the expression to demonstrate this.

Question 3

Ollie is 5 years older than Jamie. Jamie is *X* years older than David. David is *Z* years old.

Write the expression to show how old Ollie is.

Question 4

Ellie bakes 6 loaves of bread (*B*) per day. She also makes 22 cupcakes (*C*) per day.

Write the expression to show how many loaves of bread and number of cupcakes Ellie makes per week.

Question 5

A recipe for soup contains 4 carrots (*C*) and 3 tomatoes (*T*). This recipe serves 4 people.

Write the expression to show the ingredients needed to serve soup for 12 people.

Question 6

Rachel spends *Y* amount on petrol per month. She also pays *Z* amount per month for her car insurance.

Write the expression to show the amount that Rachel spends in 6 months.

ANSWERS TO ALGEBRA - FORMING EXPRESSIONS

Q1. $A - 6$

EXPLANATION = if Sammie loses 6 marbles, the total would be A (total number of marbles) subtract 6 (the amount Sammie has lost).

Q2. $2b + 28f$

EXPLANATION = Lalita needs to buy two beds, one for each cat ($2b$ = 2 x beds). Lalita also needs to buy 14 packets of food per cat, which means she needs to buy 28 packets in total for the week ($28f$ = 28 x packets of food).

Q3. $Z + x + 5$

EXPLANATION = Z is David's age. Jamie is Y years older than David ($Z + Y$). Ollie is 5 years older than David ($Z + Y + 5$)

Q4. $42b + 154c$

EXPLANATION = in a week, Ellie bakes 42 loaves of bread (6 per day). She makes 22 cupcakes per day, which is equivalent to 154 per week.
So $42B$ (42 x loaves of bread, per week) + $154C$ (154 x cupcakes, per week).

Q5. $12c + 9t$

EXPLANATION = you need 3 times as many ingredients to cater for 12 people. So 4 carrots x 3 = 12 carrots ($12c$).
3 tomatoes x 3 = 9 tomatoes ($9t$).
$12c + 9t$

Q6. $6y + 6z$

EXPLANATION = 6 x the amount of petrol = $6y$.
6 x the amount of car insurance = $6z$.
$6y + 6z$

HOW ARE YOU GETTING ON?

ALGEBRA – SIMPLIFYING EQUATIONS

ALGEBRA – SIMPLIFYING EQUATIONS

REARRANGING EQUATIONS

In order to simplify equations and expressions, we need to **rearrange** the terms, so that all the letters are on one side of the equation, and all the numbers are on the other side.

To simplify equations and expressions:

- We need to collect together '**like terms**'.
- Like terms are basically another way of describing the same terms (i.e. collecting all the x terms, or collecting all the numbers).

LETTERS ON ONE SIDE OF THE EQUATION AND NUMBERS ON THE OTHER!

The best way to demonstrate how you collect like terms, and simplify equations, is by using an example:

EXAMPLE

Simplify the following expression

$$5x + 9x - 3 - 2x + 7$$

Step 1 = first you need to break up the equation. Remember the operations in the equation will remain on the left side.

$$(5x)\ (+\ 9x)\ (-\ 3)\ (-\ 2x)\ (+\ 7)$$

Step 2 = you want to group the numbers together and group the letters together.

$$(5x)\ (+\ 9x)\ (-\ 3)\ (-\ 2x)\ (+\ 7)$$
$$(5x + 9x - 2x) = 12x$$
$$(-3 + 7) = 4$$
$$\textbf{12x + 4}$$

Step 3 = so the expression you started with, can be simplified to **12x + 4**.

For the following questions, simplify the equations.

Question 1

$r + r + r + r + r =$

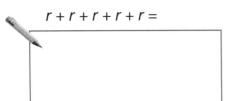

Question 2

$d + g + g + d =$

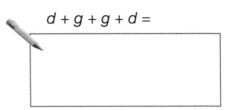

Question 3

$h + h + h - h =$

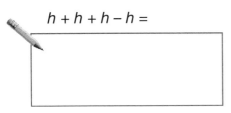

Question 4

$2k + 3k + 4g - 3g =$

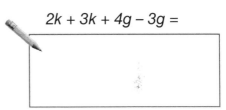

Question 5

$a + c + b + 2c + 3a - 2 =$

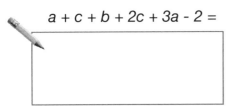

Question 6

$t^2 + 5c + 4s - c + 2s =$

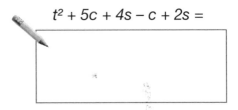

Question 7

$4x + 4y - 2x - 3y =$

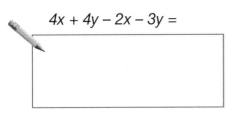

Question 8

$4 + 2 + 3c - 2y - c =$

Question 9

$n \times n \times n =$

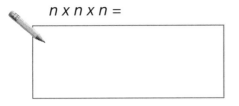

Question 10

$2a + 3y + 5 + 6a =$

ANSWERS TO ALGEBRA – SIMPLIFYING EQUATIONS

Q1. 5r

EXPLANATION $= r + r + r + r + r = 5r$ (there are 5 'r' terms in the equation).

Q2. 2d + 2g

EXPLANATION = (d) (+ g) (+ g) (+ d)

(d + d) = 2d

(g + g) = 2g

2d + 2g

Q3. 2h

EXPLANATION = (h) (+ h) (+ h) (- h)

(h + h + h) = 3h

3h (-h) = 2h

Q4. 5k + 1g

EXPLANATION = (2k) (+ 3k) (+ 4g) (- 3g)

(2k + 3k) = 5k

(4g – 3g) = 1g

5k + 1g

Q5. 4a + 3c + b - 2

EXPLANATION = (a) (+ c) (+ b) (+ 2c) (+ 3a) (- 2)

(a + 3a) = 4a

(c + 2c) = 3c

(+b – 2)

4a + 3c + b – 2

Q6. t² + 4c + 6s

EXPLANATION = (t²) (+ 5c) (+ 4s) (- c) (+ 2s)

(t²)

(5c – c) = 4c

$(4s + 2s) = 6s$

$t^2 + 4c + 6s$

Q7. 2x + 1y

EXPLANATION $= (4x) (+ 4y) (- 2x) (- 3y)$

$(4x - 2x) = 2x$

$(4y - 3y) = 1y$

$2x + 1y$

Q8. 6 + 2c – 2y

EXPLANATION $= (4) (+ 2) (+ 3c) (- 2y) (- c)$

$(4 + 2) = 6$

$(3c - c) = 2c$

$(-2y)$

$6 + 2c - 2y$

Q9. n³

EXPLANATION $= (n) (\times n) (\times n) = (n^3)$

Q10. 8a + 3y + 5

EXPLANATION $= (2a) (+ 3y) (+ 5) (+ 6a)$

$(2a + 6a) = 8a$

$(+ 3y + 5)$

$8a + 3y + 5$

HOW ARE YOU GETTING ON?

ALGEBRA —
NUMBER
SEQUENCES

ALGEBRA – NUMBER SEQUENCES

SEQUENCES AND PATTERNS

Sometimes you may be asked to work out a number sequence. These are relatively simple if you know how the sequence is progressing.

There are 6 different ways the number sequences could be presented to you.

- Before we move on to finding a number in the sequence, let's quickly take a look at some of the ways in which the number sequences might be progressing.

1. ADDING THE SAME NUMBER

Number sequences may be progressing by ADDING the SAME number.

The best way to see how the sequence is progressing, is to write down the differences between each of the numbers.

$$1 \quad 10 \quad 19 \quad 28 \quad 37 \quad ...$$

$$+9 \quad +9 \quad +9 \quad +9$$

So the rule for this sequence is **ADD 9**.

2. SUBTRACTING THE SAME NUMBER

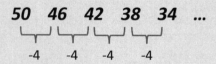

Number sequences may be progressing by SUBTRACTING the SAME number.

$$50 \quad 46 \quad 42 \quad 38 \quad 34 \quad ...$$

$$-4 \quad -4 \quad -4 \quad -4$$

So the rule for this sequence is **SUBTRACT 4**.

ALGEBRA – NUMBER SEQUENCES

3. MULTIPLY THE SAME NUMBER

Number sequences may be progressing by MULTIPLYING the SAME number.

$$3 \quad 6 \quad 12 \quad 24 \quad 48 \quad \ldots$$

x2   x2   x2   x2

So the rule for this sequence is **MULTILPYING 2**.

4. DIVIDE THE SAME NUMBER

Number sequences may be progressing by DIVIDING the SAME number.

$$800 \quad 400 \quad 200 \quad 100 \quad 50 \quad \ldots$$

÷2   ÷2   ÷2   ÷2

So the rule for this sequence is **DIVIDE 2**.

5. ADD OR SUBTRACT DIFFERENT NUMBERS

Number sequences may be progressing by ADDING or SUBTRACTING different numbers.

$$1 \quad 3 \quad 6 \quad 10 \quad 15 \quad \ldots$$

+2   +3   +4   +5

So the rule for this sequence is **ADD 1 EXTRA TO THE PREVIOUS TERM**.

$$40 \quad 34 \quad 29 \quad 25 \quad 22 \quad \ldots$$

-6   -5   -4   -3

So the rule for this sequence is **SUBTRACT 1 EXTRA TO THE PREVIOUS TERM**.

6. ADDING THE PREVIOUS TERMS TOGETHER

Number sequences may be progressing by ADDING THE PREVIOUS TERMS TOGETHER

$$3 \quad 4 \quad 7 \quad 11 \quad 18 \quad ...$$

$$3+4 \quad 4+7 \quad 7+11$$

So the rule for this sequence is **ADDING THE TWO PREVIOUS TERMS**.

Now that you have a good understanding of the different types of number sequence, you can now move on to slightly harder questions.

Sometimes you may be given a number sequence, and the question will ask you to *'find the 300ᵗʰ term in the sequence'*.

If you were to work it out using the above examples, it would take forever!

On the next page we have demonstrated the quickest method that you can use to answer these types of question. Read through these examples carefully, before having a go at some practice questions.

ALGEBRA – NUMBER SEQUENCES

FINDING THE Nth TERM

When it comes to numbers and sequences, there is a simple rule that you can use to work out the number in any sequence.

The rule for any number sequence:

> To find the next term i.e. the next number in a patterned sequence, you can use the algebra term **n** in order to represent the number you are trying to find.

EXAMPLE 1

Find the 100th term in the following sequence:

$$4, \quad 11, \quad 18, \quad 25, \quad 32 \; ...$$

Step 1 = first, you need to work out how the sequence is progressing.

1st term	2nd term	3rd term	4th term	5th term
4	11	18	25	32

    +7   +7   +7   +7

Step 2 = as you can see, you are adding 7. So the rule for this sequence is 7n. However, the first term (4) is too small for this rule to work, so therefore the rule needs to be changed to the following:

    7n – 3

Step 3 = check that this new rule, works for the sequence. Let's take the 4th term:

    4 x 7 = 28 – 3 = 25

Step 4 = now that you know this rule works, let's find the 100th term:

    100 x 7 = 700 – 3 = 697

Step 5 = so the 100th term in this sequence is **697**.

ALGEBRA – NUMBER SEQUENCES

EXAMPLE 2

Find the 300th term in the following sequence:

5, 10, 15, 20, 25 ...

Step 1 = first, you need to work out how the sequence is progressing.

1st term	2nd term	3rd term	4th term	5th term
5	10	15	20	25

+5   +5   +5   +5

Step 2 = as you can see, you are adding 5.

Step 3 = So the rule for this sequence is $5n$ ($5 \times n$).

Step 4 = so the 300th term in this sequence would be $5 \times 300 = 15{,}000$.

Step 5 = so the 300th term in this sequence is **15,000**.

Now you try!

Find the 100th term in the following sequence:

8   17   26   35   44

Question 1

Write the next 5 terms in the following number sequence.

1st term	2nd term	3rd term	4th term	5th term
9	18	27	36	45

6th term	7th term	8th term	9th term	10th term

Question 2

Write the next 5 terms in the following number sequence.

1st term	2nd term	3rd term	4th term	5th term
7	12	17	22	27

6th term	7th term	8th term	9th term	10th term

Question 3

Write the next 5 terms in the following number sequence.

1st term	2nd term	3rd term	4th term	5th term
208	197	186	175	164

6th term	7th term	8th term	9th term	10th term

Question 4

Lalita needs your help! She is stuck with the following number sequence.

| 1 | 2 | 3 | 4 |

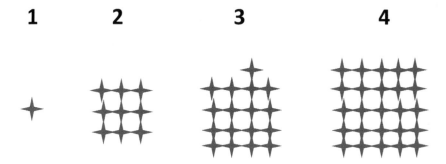

Complete the table to show how many diamonds are needed to complete each diagram.

Pattern number (n)	1st	2nd	3rd	4th	5th	6th	7th
Number of diamonds (d)	1	9	17				

Question 5

You have now worked out the first 7 terms in the above sequence. Using the above sequence, what would the 100th term be? After you have written out your answer, also write the rule you used to reach the correct answer.

ANSWER=

(n) = pattern number and (d) = number of diamonds.

RULE:

Question 6

Write down the general rule for the following sequence. Use the term n to represent the term of the sequence.

$$4 \quad 8 \quad 12 \quad 16 \quad ...$$

Question 7

Write down the general rule for the following sequence. Use the term n to represent the term of the sequence.

$$100 \quad 95 \quad 90 \quad 85 \quad ...$$

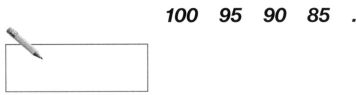

Question 8

Write down the general rule for the following sequence. Use the term n to represent the term of the sequence.

$$1.5 \quad 2.5 \quad 3.5 \quad 4.5 \quad ...$$

Question 9

What is the 18th term in the sequence, if the rule is $4n - 4$? The n represents the term in the sequence.

Question 10

Work out the *n*th term in the following sequence:

$$3 \quad 6 \quad 9 \quad 12 \quad \ldots$$

Question 11

Work out the *10*th term in the following sequence:

$$4 \quad 8 \quad 12 \quad 16 \quad \ldots$$

Question 12

Lalita has created the following expression: $8n + 11$. If n represents the *n*th term in the sequence, what would the 60th term in the sequence be?

ANSWERS TO ALGEBRA – NUMBER SEQUENCES

Q1. Your answer should look like this:

6th term	7th term	8th term	9th term	10th term
54	63	72	81	90

Q2. Your answer should look like this:

6th term	7th term	8th term	9th term	10th term
32	37	42	47	52

Q3. Your answer should look like this:

6th term	7th term	8th term	9th term	10th term
153	142	131	120	109

Q4. Your answer should look like this:

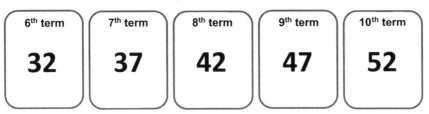

Pattern number (n)	1st	2nd	3rd	4th	5th	6th	7th
Number of diamonds (d)	1	9	17	25	33	41	49

Q5. Your answer should look like this:

8 x 100 = 800

800 − 7 = 793

ANSWER=   **793**

(n) = pattern number and (d) = number of diamonds.

RULE: Number of diamonds = (8 x *n*) − 7

Q6. 4*n*

EXPLANATION = the sequence progresses in multiples of 4. To find the nth term, you would need to multiply the term that you are trying to find (i.e. the 7th term in the sequence) by 4 (because the sequence is multiples of 4).

Q7. 100 − (*n* − 1) x 5

EXPLANATION = let's use this rule and see if it works:

To find the 2nd term: (2 − 1 = 1) x 5 = 5.   So, 100 − 5 = 95.

This rule works, as 95 is the 2nd term in the sequence.

Q8. n + 0.5

EXPLANATION = n is the term that you are trying to find. So, the 2nd term in the sequence is 2 + 0.5 = 2.5.

Q9. 68

EXPLANATION = 4 x 18 (18th term) = 72 − 4 = 68

Q10. 3*n*

EXPLANATION = the sequence progresses by 3 each time, so to work out the next term, you need to multiply the term by 3 = 3 x *n*.

Q11. 40

EXPLANATION = n = 10 (10th term). The sequence is progressing by 4, so 4 x 10 = 40.

Q12. 491

EXPLANATION = 8 x 60 = 480 + 11 = 491

HOW ARE YOU GETTING ON?